INVESTIGATING SPACE

Our Moon

Anne Cohen
Photographs by Robert Pickett

Contents

A & C Black · London

What is the Moon?

Earth's Moon is a grey ball of rock measuring about 3500 kilometres across. This is what the Moon looks like close-up. The grey rock does not make any light of its own, but the Moon looks bright in the night sky because it has sunshine falling on it. It reflects sunlight back to us on Earth. There is no air or water on the Moon, so nothing can live there.

Some of the other planets have moons, too. These can be
made of rock, or a mixture of rock and ice. Earth has only
one moon, but planets such as Saturn, Neptune and
Jupiter have many. This is a photograph of Jupiter with
two of its moons, red Io and pale Europa.

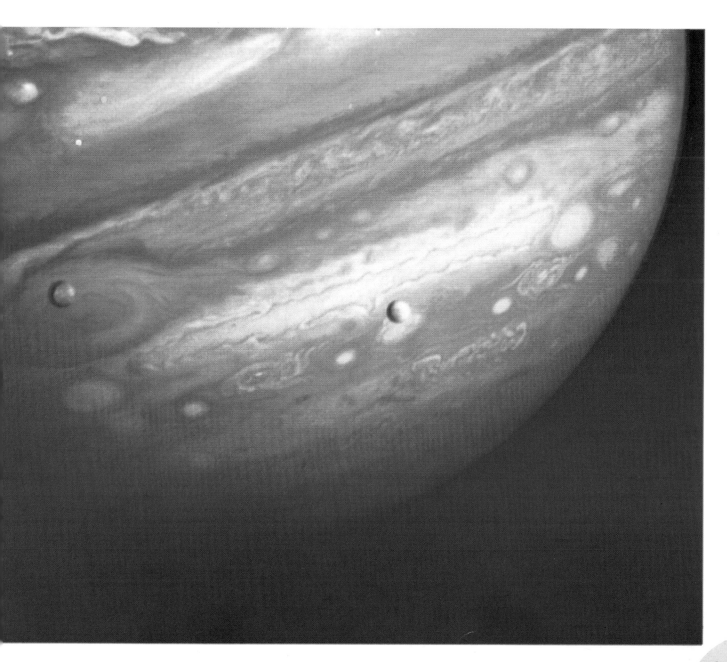

The Moon's changing shape

Can you see the Moon in the sky tonight? What shape is it?
Have you noticed how sometimes it's a thin, curved crescent
and at other times it's a brilliant, round 'full' Moon?
Sometimes the Moon is hidden behind clouds, or you can't
see it at all, even if the sky is clear.

If you keep a chart of how the Moon looks each night you will find something out. Keep watching for five or six weeks. Draw the shape of the Moon in each square of your chart. If it's too cloudy or foggy to see the Moon, make a note of this on the chart. Don't forget to look in the morning sky too.

Can you spot a pattern in the Moon's changing shape? Does the pattern repeat itself after about four weeks?

Sunday	Monday	Tuesday	Wednesday	Thursday	Friday	Saturday
			8/11	9/11	10/11	11/11
5/11	6/11	7/11	14/11	15/11	16/11	18/11
12/11	13/11				17/11	
19/11	20/11	21/11	22/11	23/11	24/11	

Try this investigation to find out why the Moon seems to change shape during the month. Use a white or a grey ball on a stick to be the Moon. Your head is the Earth. The Earth spins round once every 24 hours. Your head cannot spin round but your eyes can see an Earth-based view of the Moon. Use a light to represent the Sun.

Hold up the Moon in the light like this. The light is the Sun shining on the Earth and the Moon. Which part of the Moon looks bright to you?

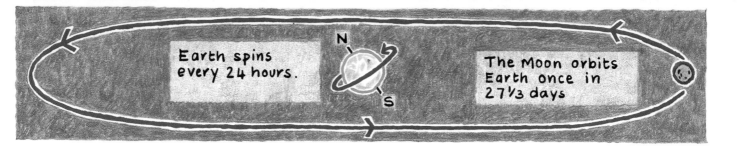

Earth spins every 24 hours.

N
S

The Moon orbits Earth once in 27⅓ days

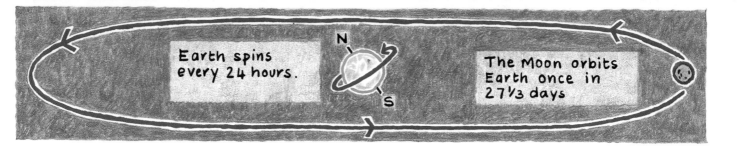

The Moon moves round the Earth, taking about a month to complete the circle. To show this, turn slowly on the spot so that the Moon moves in a circle round your head. The Moon goes round the Earth in an anticlockwise direction. Show this by turning to your left. As you turn, how much of the brightly-lit side of the Moon can you see?

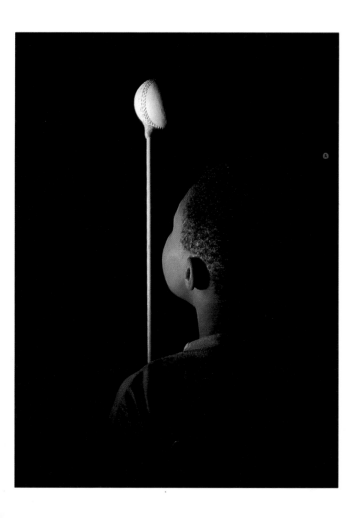

Sketching the Moon

The Moon has pale grey markings on its face. These are the flatter places on its rocky surface. People used to think that these were seas, but we now know that the Moon is very dry.

Try making a sketch of the markings that you can see on the Moon. You'll see more detail through a pair of binoculars.

Be careful if you look at a full moon through binoculars. It is so bright that it may hurt your eyes.

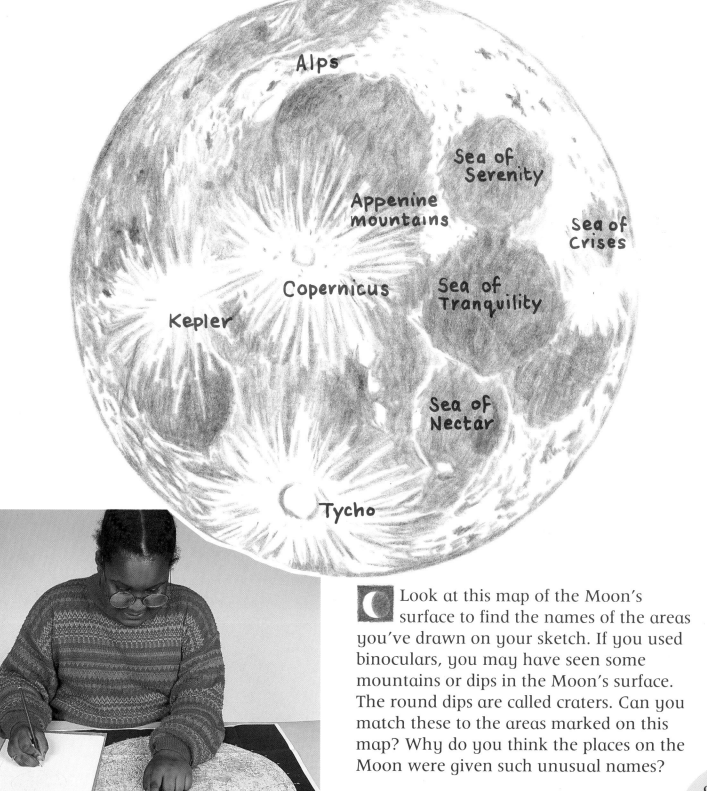

Alps

Sea of
Serenity

Appenine
mountains

Sea of
Crises

Copernicus

Sea of
Tranquility

Kepler

Sea of
Nectar

Tycho

Look at this map of the Moon's surface to find the names of the areas you've drawn on your sketch. If you used binoculars, you may have seen some mountains or dips in the Moon's surface. The round dips are called craters. Can you match these to the areas marked on this map? Why do you think the places on the Moon were given such unusual names?

The Moon's far side

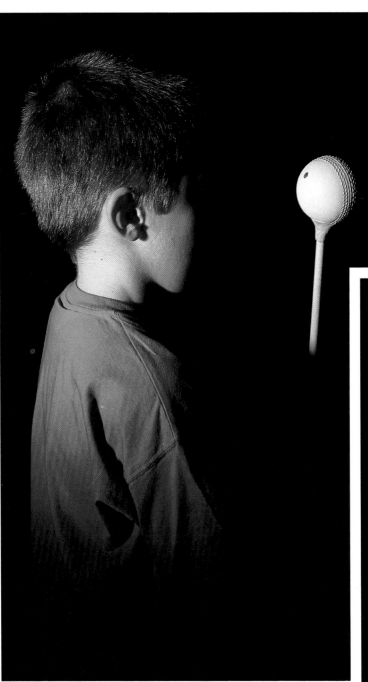

The same side of the Moon is turned towards the Earth all the time. You can see how this happens by drawing a crater on one side of your model Moon. Keep the crater facing towards you as you turn round once. Remember to turn to your left. You can always see the crater you've drawn, but you never see the other side of the Moon.

Nobody knew what the far side of the Moon looked like until spacecraft visited it. This photograph was taken in 1969 by the astronauts on board Apollo 10. It shows that the far side of the Moon is grey and cratered too, much like the side that we can see from Earth.

What are eclipses?

The Moon orbits, or goes round, the Earth. Sometimes the Moon moves in front of the Sun and blocks out the sunlight to Earth. It makes a round shadow on the Earth's surface. Someone standing at this place on Earth would see the Sun completely blocked out as it is in the picture. This is called a solar eclipse.

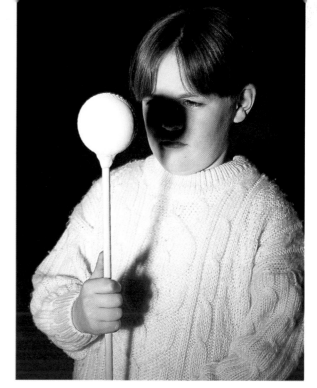

To see how a solar eclipse happens, hold up your model Moon as in the picture on the right, so that it casts a shadow on to your face. Remember that your head is the Earth.

Another sort of eclipse can happen when the Earth is between the Moon and the Sun. Turn slowly on the spot as in the picture below so that the model Moon goes round half of its orbit. Now the Moon is in the shadow of your head. In this position, the Earth is stopping light from the Sun reaching the Moon. The Moon goes dark for an hour or so until it moves further along its orbit and the Sun can shine on it again.

This photograph shows the Earth's shadow falling on the Moon. This is a lunar eclipse. The Moon looks dark orange.

Travelling to the Moon

In 1969 astronauts landed on the Moon's surface for the first time. They left Earth in the Apollo 11 spacecraft. The spacecraft was lifted into space by a huge rocket called the Saturn 5.

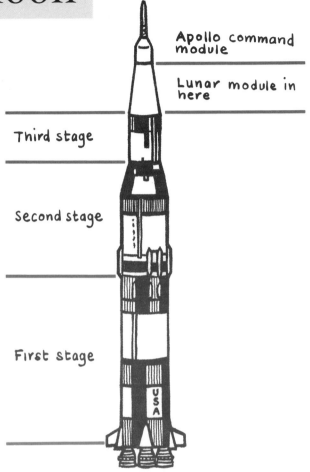

Apollo command module

Lunar module in here

Third stage

Second stage

First stage

The rocket was built in three stages. Sections in each of the three stages stored the huge amount of fuel that was needed to launch the rocket on its journey to the Moon. Each section separated from the rest of the rocket as the fuel in it was used up.

The section which returned to Earth was called the command module. The astronauts lived and worked in this section of the Apollo spacecraft.

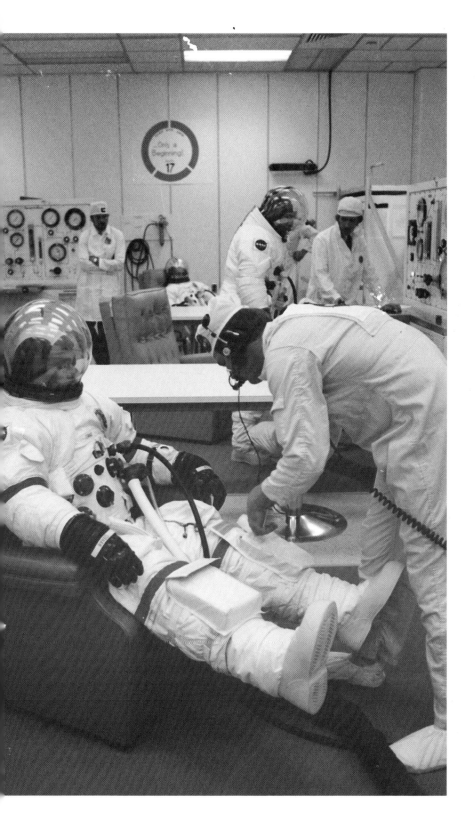

For their journey to the Moon the astronauts needed special equipment, including space suits, helmets and air tanks. There is no air to breathe on the Moon or in space, so they had to take their own supply of air .

The special suits protected the astronauts against the fierce changes of temperature on the Moon's surface. During lunar day, when the Sun is shining on the Moon, the surface reaches a temperature of 110°C.

During the lunar night, when the Moon's surface receives none of the Sun's light, the surface is colder than the inside of a freezer.

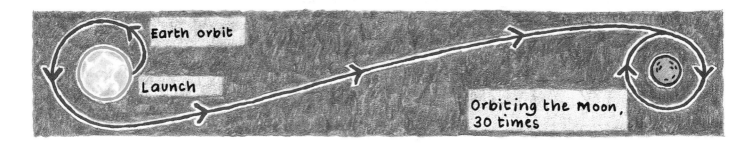

Earth orbit

Launch

Orbiting the Moon, 30 times

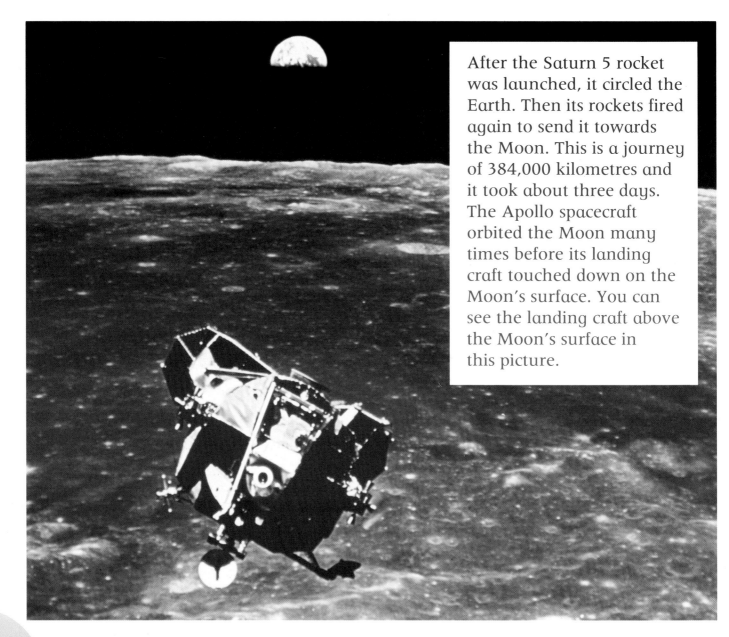

After the Saturn 5 rocket was launched, it circled the Earth. Then its rockets fired again to send it towards the Moon. This is a journey of 384,000 kilometres and it took about three days. The Apollo spacecraft orbited the Moon many times before its landing craft touched down on the Moon's surface. You can see the landing craft above the Moon's surface in this picture.

How was the spacecraft able to travel in a circle round the Earth and the Moon? You can investigate this by making a model rocket out of card. Put a small piece of plasticine inside the rocket to make it slightly heavier. Fasten a piece of thread to the side of the rocket. Then you can whirl the rocket round your head.

Why do you need a piece of thread to make it travel in a circle? Can you feel the pull that your hand makes on the thread? What happens if the thread snaps suddenly?

The Apollo spacecraft used the pull of gravity to keep it going in a circle as it orbited the Moon.

Investigating gravity

 Gravity is a force which pulls everything down towards Earth. You can see the effect of gravity if you push some objects off a table top or jump down off a chair. Gravity gives you your weight.

The Moon has gravity too, but because the Moon is much smaller than the Earth, the pull of gravity on the Moon is less. The astronauts felt much lighter on the Moon because there was less pull. They walked in large, kangaroo hops and jumped much higher than they could have done on Earth.

The astronauts were able to see for themselves that the pull of gravity on the Moon is less than it is on Earth. Whenever they dropped something, they noticed that it fell much more slowly than it would do on Earth.

The Moon's surface

The rocky surface of the Moon is covered with a fine, grey dust. Because there is no wind to blow the dust about, the clear boot prints made by the astronauts' boots are still there today.

The astronauts carried out many experiments on the Moon's surface. These included an investigation of rock tremors which the astronauts called 'Moonquakes'. They collected samples of rock which were later studied by scientists on Earth. The astronauts drove around in a special car called a Lunar Rover which was built to work on the surface of the Moon.

You can design a Lunar Rover. Remember, it doesn't have to be very strong because everything weighs less on the Moon. But it has to be able to drive over rocky ground and through dust. Test your Lunar Rover on a surface of fine sand.

The surface of the Moon is covered with craters. The largest are over 100 kilometres across and the smallest are very tiny. Most of the craters were made millions of years ago by pieces of rock which crashed into the Moon's surface. These rocks were drifting about in the Solar System. When they came near to the Moon, the force of gravity pulled them down on to its surface.

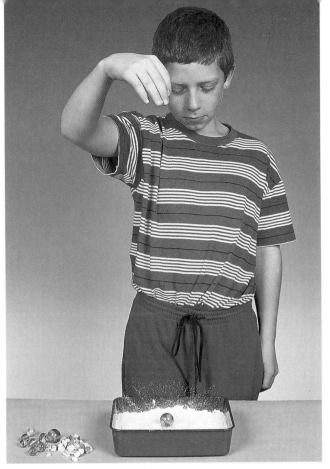

You can try making craters in a surface of fine flour. Drop small pebbles or marbles into the flour and see what shape holes they make.

Craters have been made on the Earth's surface, too. These children are holding a piece of rock which fell to Earth in 1879 and landed in Bovedy in Northern Ireland. The rock is very heavy as it is made mostly of iron. Rocks like this one which crash into the Earth's surface are called meteorites.

Notes for teachers and parents

As you share this book with children, these notes will help you to get the most from the investigations.

The Moon's changing shape (pages 4, 5, 6, 7)

Keeping a Moon diary (page 4) requires careful regular observations over a six-week period and some encouragement may be needed. On many days the Moon will not be seen because of cloudy weather. Note that a technical 'New Moon' is not visible even in a clear sky, since the whole of the earthward side is dark. The thin crescent only shows in the evening sky a day or two AFTER the date of 'New Moon'. Remember to look for the waning Moon in the morning sky. During the second half of the lunar cycle, the Moon is still up after sunrise and so may be visible at breakfast time, or on the way to school.

The investigation using a ball on a stick for the Moon (pages 6, 7) will only show the correct series of phases to the person holding the stick, and so each child will need to try the activity for themselves. Only the person holding the model Moon has the Earth's view of the Moon. Everyone else in the room will see phases, but they will be as seen from outer space!

Any strong direct light can be used to represent sunlight – this could be provided for example by a slide projector or an overhead projector.

Sketching the Moon (pages 8, 9)

As an extension activity, the children could find out more about the astronomers, mathematicians and scientists after whom the lunar craters are named.

What are eclipses? (pages 12, 13)

This activity might imply that eclipses happen every month as the Moon orbits the Earth. This will happen in the activity if the model Moon is moved in a circle level with the child's head. In fact the Moon's orbit is inclined to the Earth-Sun direction, and so the Moon does not always pass directly between Earth and Sun. You can show this with the model by holding the 'Moon' a little higher for one half of its orbit and a little lower for the other half.

Travelling to the Moon (pages 16, 17)

Choose strong string for the model rocket activity, and stand away from onlookers so that the model does not hit them.

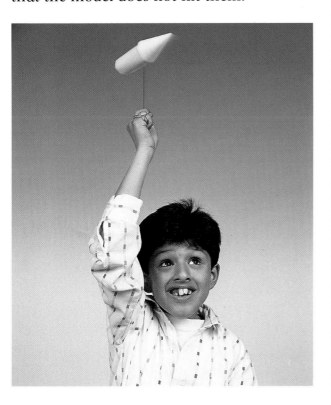

The Moon's surface (pages 20, 21, 22, 23)

Suggested materials for a Lunar Rover: cotton reels, egg boxes, straws, empty food packets, corrugated cardboard, the centres of kitchen rolls or toilet rolls. Pieces from manufactured building kits can also be used.

Craters in flour sometimes look more realistic if the flour has been sifted into the tray or dish.

Index